Building Better RELATIONSHIPS

Bobbie Yagel

Gospel Light

AGLOW
INTERNATIONAL

Gospel Light is an evangelical Christian publisher dedicated to serving the local church. We believe God's vision for Gospel Light is to provide church leaders with biblical, user-friendly materials that will help them evangelize, disciple and minister to children, youth and families.

We hope this Gospel Light resource will help you discover biblical truth for your own life and help you minister to adults. God bless you in your work.

For a free catalog of resources from Gospel Light please contact your Christian supplier or contact us at 1-800-4-GOSPEL or at www.gospellight.com.

PUBLISHING STAFF
William T. Greig, Publisher
Dr. Elmer L. Towns, Senior Consulting Publisher
Dr. Gary S. Greig, Senior Consulting Editor
Jill Honodel, Editor
Pam Weston, Assistant Editor
Kyle Duncan, Associate Publisher
Bayard Taylor, M.Div., Senior Editor, Theological and Biblical Issues
Barbara LeVan Fisher, Cover Designer
Debi Thayer, Designer

Aglow International is an interdenominational organization of Christian women. Our mission is to lead women to Jesus Christ and provide opportunity for Christian women to grow in their faith and minister to others.

Our publications are used to help women find a personal relationship with Jesus Christ, to enhance growth in their Christian experience, and to help them recognize their roles and relationships according to Scripture.

For more information about our organization, please write to Aglow International, P.O. Box 1749, Edmonds, WA 98020-1749, U.S.A., or call (425) 775-7282. For ordering or information about the Aglow studies call (800) 793-8126.

CONTENTS

Chapter One

Chapter Two

Chapter Three

Chapter Four

Chapter Five

Chapter Six

Chapter Seven

Chapter Eight

DEDICATION

This book is dedicated to:

Myron, the love of my life, who graces me
with love and acceptance;

Our adult children: Craig, Stephen and Wendy,
constant sources of love, joy and pride;

Our daughter-in-law Denise and son-in-law Jeff,
who fit so beautifully into our family;

Our grandchildren, Amber, Devin, Brandon and Daniel,
our delights, so easy to adore and cherish.

OREWORD

When the apostle Paul poured out his heart in letters to the young churches in Asia, he was responding to his apostolic call to shepherd those tender flocks. They needed encouragement in their new life in Jesus. They needed solid doctrine. They needed truth from someone who had an intimate relationship with God and with them.

Did Paul know as he was writing that these simple letters would form the bulk of the New Testament? We can be confident that the Holy Spirit did! How like God to use Paul's relationship with these churches to cement His plan and purpose in their lives, and, generations later, in ours.

We in Aglow can relate to Paul's desire to bond those young churches together in the faith. After 1967, when Aglow fellowships began bubbling up across the United States and in other countries, they needed encouragement. They needed to know the fullness of who they were in Christ. They needed relationship. Like Paul, our desire to reach out and nurture from far away birthed a series of Bible studies that have fed thousands since 1973 when our first study, *Genesis*, was published. Our studies share heart-to-heart, giving Christians new insights about themselves and their relationship with and in God.

God's generous nature has recently provided us a rewarding new relationship with Gospel Light Publications. Together we are publishing our Aglow classics, as well as a selection of exciting new studies. Gospel Light began as a publishing ministry much in the same way Aglow began publishing Bible studies. Henrietta Mears, one of its visionary founders, formed Gospel Light in response to requests from churches across America for the Sunday School materials she had written for the First Presbyterian Church in Hollywood, California. Gospel Light remains a strong ministry-minded witness for the gospel around the world.

Our heart's desire is that these studies will continue to kindle the minds of women and men, touch their hearts, and refresh spirits with the light and life a loving Savior abundantly supplies.

This study, *Building Better Relationships* by Bobbie Yagel, will show you how to develop and maintain relationships based on God's love and forgiveness. I know its contents will reward you richly.

Jane Hansen
International President
Aglow International

PREFACE

The Bible describes two types of relationships, vertical and horizontal. These are best defined by John, the beloved disciple, who wrote, "We love because he first loved us. If anyone says, 'I love God,' yet hates his brother, he is a liar. For anyone who does not love his brother, whom he has seen, cannot love God, whom he has not seen. And he has given us this command: Whoever loves God must also love his brother" (1 John 4:19-21).

In the fifth chapter of 1 John, the apostle rivets our attention to the interdependence of the love of God and the love of neighbor. He wrote: "This is how we know that we love the children of God: by loving God and carrying out his commands" (1 John 5:2). Like the vertical and horizontal arms of the cross, our lives must illustrate a love for God and a love for others.

Our primary relationship is with God—all other relationships flow out from it. We must understand who we are in the Beloved—that God actually died to give us royal lineage and make us members of the family of heaven. When we truly accept this, believe this, and become established in this truth, our security is in our relationship with Jesus Christ. Then, in the security of that relationship, we are empowered to reach out and build right relationships.

—Bobbie Yagel

NTRODUCTION

In the Bible, relationship rifts multiplied as fast as the earth's population: Adam and Eve refused to accept responsibility for their sin, blaming each other and the serpent; Cain murdered his brother Abel in a fit of jealous rage; Sarah mistreated and banished her slave Hagar; Jacob stole Esau's birthright and fled for his life; Laban cheated Jacob by giving him Leah for his wife instead of the promised Rachel; and Joseph's jealous brothers sold him into slavery. And these are only a few examples from the *first* book of the Bible.

The New Testament honestly reports: Jesus' disciples tried to outmaneuver each other for the place of honor at Jesus' side; doctrinal differences in the first-century church erupted with an intensity that forced the disciples to call a conference in Jerusalem to settle escalating disputes; and Paul and Barnabas separated because of a disagreement over Mark's dependability as a missionary.

In light of these biblical examples, should we be surprised when our personal relationships sour? What we need to learn most of all is how to restore broken relationships and how to build right relationships.

Former Senate Chaplain Richard Halverson once described Christian fellowship as "coming together like grapes—crushed, with skins of ego broken, the ripe, fragrant juices of life mingling in the wine of sharing and understanding and caring." It sounds so good, so warm, so right—except that bit about the skins of ego being broken. Could the culprit of our relationship problems be the self that resists death?

Relationships are indeed the joy and the bane of the Christian life. In fellowship we receive support, encouragement, acceptance, help and love. But in fellowship we also experience rejection, judgment, discouragement, insensitivity and jealousy. Friends forsake us. Family members disappoint us. Gossip runs rampant in the church. We are often reminded that the Christian body is the only army that shoots its wounded. The Bible repeatedly reminds us that the only cure for damaged relationships is to love as Jesus loves us—unconditionally! This challenge strikes at the heart of where we live: in our homes, our neighborhoods, our churches and our places of employment.

This study tackles such nitty gritty questions as: Do we talk with the person who is gossiping about us? Do we forgive those who refuse to ask for forgiveness or admit they're wrong? How can we communicate with angry relatives without adding fuel to the fire?

Our relationships will be right to the extent we take up our cross daily to die to self, grow in grace and let Christ be more fully formed in each of us. His ways bring healing, restore peace and promote love.

If your heart hungers after right relationships, you'll find the secrets in *Building Better Relationships*.

AN OVERVIEW OF THE STUDY

This Bible study is divided into four sections:

- A CLOSER LOOK AT THE PROBLEM defines the problem and the goal of the study.
- A CLOSER LOOK AT GOD'S TRUTH gets you into God's Word. What does God have to say about the problem? How can you begin to apply God's Word as you work through each lesson?
- A CLOSER LOOK AT MY OWN HEART will help you clarify and further apply truth. It will also give guidance as you work toward change.
- ACTION STEPS I CAN TAKE TODAY is designed to help you concentrate on immediate steps of action.

You Will Need

- A Bible.
- A notebook. During this study you will want to keep a journal to record what God shows you personally. You may also want to journal additional thoughts or feelings that come up as you go through the lessons. Some questions may require more space than is given in this study book.
- Time to meditate on what you're learning. Only through meditation will you hear God's Word for you and begin to experience a heart knowledge, as well as a head knowledge, of the subject of building better relationships. Allow time for this to happen.

HOW TO START AND LEAD A SMALL GROUP

One key to starting and leading a small group is to ask yourself, what would Jesus do and how would He do it? Jesus began His earthly ministry with a small group called the disciples, and the fact of His presence made wherever He was a safe place to be. Think of a small group as a safe place. It is a place that reflects God's heart, God's hands. The way in which Jesus lived and worked with His disciples is a basic small group model that we are able to draw both direction and nurture from.

Paul exhorted us to "walk in love, as Christ also has loved us and given Himself for us" (Ephesians 5:2, *NKJV*). We, as His earthly reflections, are privileged to walk in His footsteps, to help bind up the brokenhearted as He did or simply to listen with a compassionate heart. Whether you use this book as a Bible study, or as a focus point for a support group, a church or home group, walking in love means that we "bear one another's burdens" (Galatians 6:2, *NKJV*). The loving atmosphere provided by a small group can nourish, sustain and lift us up as nothing else does.

Jesus walked in love and spoke from an honest heart. In His endless well of compassion He never misplaced truth. Rather, He surrounded it with mercy. Those who left His presence felt good about themselves because Jesus used truth to point them in the right direction for their lives. When He spoke about the sinful woman who washed Jesus' feet with her tears and wiped them with her hair, He did not deny her sin. He said, "her sins, which are many, are forgiven, for she loved much" (Luke 7:47, *NKJV*). That's honesty without condemnation.

Jesus was a model of servant leadership. "Whoever desires to become great among you shall be your servant. And whoever of you desires to be first shall be slave of all" (Mark 10:43,44, *NKJV*). One of the key skills a group leader possesses is the ability to be an encourager of the group's members to grow spiritually. Keeping in personal contact with each member of the group, especially if one is absent, tells each one that he/she is important to the group. Other skills an effective group leader will develop are: being a good listener, guiding the discussion, as well as guiding the group to deal with any conflicts that arise within it.

Whether you're a veteran or brand new to small group leadership, virtually every group you lead will be different in personality and dynamic. The constant is the presence of Jesus Christ, and when He is at the group's center, everything else can come together.

YOU'RE INVITED!

To grow...

To develop and reach maturity; thrive; to spring up; come into existence from a source;

with a group

An assemblage of persons gathered or located together; a number of individuals considered together because of similarities;

To explore...

To investigate systematically; examine; search into or range over for the purpose of discovery;

new topics

Subjects of discussion or conversation.

Meeting on

Date _____ Time_____

Located at

Place _____

_____

Contact _____

Phone _____

Note: Feel free to fill in this page and photocopy it as an invitation to hand out or post on your church bulletin board.

– One –

BUILDING RIGHT RELATIONSHIPS

How right are your relationships? Right relationships are not only essential in the family and in the church, but also in the workplace. Many studies have shown that the primary reason people lose their jobs is because of poor relational skills. A friend of mine lost a great managerial position because she told another employee a bit of confidential news the boss had shared with her. Gossip destroys relationships in the family, church and neighborhood, as well as in the workplace.

I think of a nursing home resident who received indifferent service from the home's staff because she refused to stop barking instructions at them. I tried to help her understand the importance of good body language and a warm tone of voice. I failed. She continued to speak gruffly and the staff continued giving their indifferent help. Love shows itself in our way of speaking.

One researcher claims that he can predict with 94 percent accuracy the failure or success of any marriage. His research uncovers the five to one ratio "as long as there is five times as much positive feeling and interaction between husband and wife as there is negative, we found the marriage was likely to be stable."[1] The words we speak are all too often words of death instead of words of life (see Proverbs 18:21). The level of our love for others shows itself in the words we speak.

When someone has emotionally wounded us, we often disobey Scripture by talking to a third party instead of first talking with the person who hurt us (see Matthew 18:15). Just as unscriptural is our refusal to speak with the person we know to be hurting or upset by our behavior or words (see Matthew 5:23,24). Love means learning to listen nondefensively.

The goal of this lesson is to help you take an honest look at your relationships and to see how your relationships line up with the truth of God's "one-another" commandments.

1. How would you define a right relationship? Write out your answer before you read mine!

To me, a right relationship is an open-armed approach to every person in my life, regardless of the way he/she treats me. In such a relationship, I feel no sense of separation, no unforgiven hurts, no underlying problems I refuse to discuss or choose to ignore. I am at peace with everyone as far as it depends on me (see Romans 12:18).

2. How did your definition of a right relationship differ from mine? What things would you change in your definition or my definition and why would you make these changes?

A Closer Look at the Problem

WORKING ON OUR EMOTIONAL RESPONSES

Many of us look at a relationship rift and think first of the harm done to us. We think or say, "I'm so mad at Bill. He was my best man and he didn't even ask me to be in his wedding!" or "I can't believe she didn't speak to me in the mall when I know she saw me and looked right at me." or "I feel totally unloved by my mother. She was selfish and self-centered. Mother left me with a babysitter while she ran off to fashion shows, spas, lunches with her girlfriends or bridge games. She never had time for me. How could anyone expect me to forgive her and give her a hug when I see her? I'd be a hypocrite."

The "poor me" approach is of course self-centered as opposed to God-centered. If we focus first on God's love for us that we can never deserve or earn, we may be more willing to respond with a God-inspired request such as, "Lord, I can't give love to this person. Please fill me with your love and inspire me to do the loving thing."

The Bible concerns itself with the words we speak, the negative thoughts we refuse to give up and the actions we take or refuse to take. Love is shown by words *and* actions.

Relationship problems end in separation when we refuse to work on changing our emotional responses to those who hurt us. It is virtually impossible to feel our way to new actions. If we wait until we feel loving before talking with the offending friend, the one who slighted us or the parent who gave us less love than we think we deserve, we will probably never respond. And the fire of love and friendship will be replaced with the smoldering ashes of bitterness.

3.   Share a time when you were hurt by a family member, friend or coworker, and you let your negative feelings keep you from acting in love as commanded in God's Word. (Be sure you protect the identity of the person who injured you.)

Scripture reminds us that even the pagans love those who love them. Returning love for love is no big deal in Scripture. The challenge is to love those who hate you and use you (see Matthew 5:44).

A Closer Look at God's Truth

4.   Is Jesus commanding us to *feel* something or to *do* something in the following scriptures: Matthew 25:31-40; 1 John 3:10, 4:12,19-21?

In answering this question it is helpful to remember that the New Testament verb for love, *agapao*, is an action word. *Vine's Complete Expository Dictionary* explains, "Love can be known only from the actions it prompts. God's love is seen in the gift of His Son. 1 John 4:9,10...Love had its perfect expression among men in the Lord Jesus Christ."[2]

The Bible also uses the word *phileo* for love. This is the *feeling* word for love, best translated as "tender affections." *Phileo* is used of God's love for His Son and of God's love for us. But please note: "*Phileo* is never used in a command to men to love God."[3]

After reading the above scriptures, we can see clearly that the way we treat the least significant or most obnoxious persons in our lives is a barometer of our love for Jesus Christ. Since love is known by the actions it takes, let's look at some of the Bible's "one another" commandments to learn how our heavenly Father expects us to act.

Please look up the following references and write the key action word for each passage, such as "serve" or "forgive."

a. Romans 12:10 _____ to one another.

b. Romans 12:13 _____ with God's people.

c. Romans 12:14 _____ and do not _____.

d. Romans 15:1 _____ the failings of the weak.

e. 2 Corinthians 13:12 _____ each other.

f. Galatians 5:13 _____ one another.

g. Ephesians 5:21 _____ to one another.

h. Colossians 3:13 _____ with each other and

_____.

i. 1 Thessalonians 5:11 _____ one another and

_____ each other.

j. James 5:16 _____ for each other.

5. What are some of the reasons you find it easy or difficult to maintain right relationships in the following situations? Write down the names of specific people in your life as you answer.

    • with friends?

    • with family members?

    • in the workplace?

    • in church?

Sometimes when I read the "one-another" passages, I experience spiritual claustrophobia, a sense of too much togetherness. I prefer not to confess my sins to anyone but God. I'm not too keen on hugging, much less greeting with a kiss. I prefer hugging myself to greeting others with sisterly affection. Daily I would feel smothered by a gigantic blanket of guilt if I had to first feel like doing these things. When living in step with God, I am obedient to these "one-another" scriptures even when I feel negative about the required actions. Constantly I must remind myself: *Love is an action I take, not a sentiment I feel.*

A Closer Look at My Own Heart

Scripture tells us the heart is deceitful above all else (see Jeremiah 17:9). This is why, with prayer, we need to evaluate and discover how right our relationships are. The following test is designed to help you rate yourself in the area of relationships.

Beside each of the following behaviors place a number from one to six.

1—Almost always	4—Occasionally
2—With few exceptions	5—Rarely
3—Usually	6—Never

Choose the number from one to six that best describes your behavior in the following situations:

_____ 1. I make myself move toward a person who has hurt me, as opposed to withdrawing. To move toward means to reach out with an act of kindness, to talk to at a social event, to call on the phone, etc. (see Romans 12:18).

_____ 2. I forgive people when they hurt me, even if they do not admit their wrongs or ask to be forgiven (see Colossians 3:13).

_____ 3. I go to other people as soon as I realize I have hurt or upset them and ask to be forgiven (see Matthew 5:23,24).

_____ 4. I attribute good motives to people when they hurt me, such as "I'm sure they meant me no harm"—as opposed to deciding someone has deliberately hurt me (see 1 Corinthians 13:6,7).

_____ 5. I receive criticism without attacking the person criticizing me and/or without defending myself (see Matthew 5:11).

_____ 6. I share what is good and helpful for building others up—as opposed to gossip and giving a bad report (see Ephesians 4:29).

_____ 7. I make my mind dwell on things that are true, pure and excellent as opposed to dwelling on the wrongs done to me (see Philippians 4:8).

_____ 8. I am quick to listen and slow to speak (see James 1:19).

_____ 9. I am careful not to judge anyone (see Matthew 7:1).

_____ 10. I practice hospitality without grumbling (see 1 Peter 4:9).

_____ 11. I consider others more important than myself and am happy to let another car move in front of me or to give up my plans for the day in order to serve another (see Philippians 2:3).

_____ 12. I give comfort to those hurting—as opposed to butting into the conversation with my problems, criticizing the speaker for his or her feelings or making light of the other's problems (see Romans 12:15).

_____ 13. I confess my faults to at least one other Christian (see James 5:16).

_____ 14. I receive all people warmly and affectionately, even if they are poor, needy, repetitious, in need of a bath, boring or obnoxious (see Romans 15:7, James 2:1).

_____ 15. I speak words of encouragement to others—as opposed to pointing out their faults (see Hebrews 3:13; 10:25).

Grading Yourself

If you have a majority of numbers from 1 to 3, you have good relationships. A majority of numbers from 4 to 6 indicate behavior that is less than God's best for you.

In what area do you most need to grow in obedience to God's relationship commandments?

Share this with one other person and pray for one another.

Action Steps I Can Take Today

Put your new attitudes into action. Choose the most troubling relationship in your life at this time. Prayerfully ask God to show you where you have failed to love this person God's way. Confess your sin.

Next, ask God the best way for you to express His love to this difficult family member, friend or acquaintance. Wait upon the Lord and listen. When you think you have heard from God, act immediately! Place the phone call, write the note, stop by with flowers, whatever action the Holy Spirit inspires.

Notes:
1. John Gottman, *Why Marriages Succeed or Fail* (New York, N.Y.: Simon & Schuster, 1994), p. 57.
2. W. E. Vine, *Vine's Complete Expository Dictionary* (Nashville, Tenn.: Thomas Nelson Inc., 1984), pp. 381-382.
3. Ibid, p. 382.

Two

LOVING OUR NEIGHBORS

I recently read a story in my hometown newspaper about a distraught man who entered the emergency room of a local hospital and announced that he planned to kill himself. A savvy secretary asked the man if he loved himself. When the man said no, the secretary replied, "If you are here, asking for help, it seems to me that you do love yourself."

Whenever I teach this lesson about loving our neighbors, I know I will be asked one question: "Don't I have to learn to love myself before you expect me to love others?"

My reply is always the same: "No, the problem is that you already love yourself too much."

Why would I reply so harshly when I usually don't know anything about the questioner? First of all, my answer lines up with the Bible. Secondly, nowhere in Scripture are we commanded to love ourselves. Scripture assumes we love ourselves. The goal of this chapter is to help you understand the biblical truths about loving others as much as we love ourselves.

A Closer Look at the Problem

LOVING OTHERS AS MUCH AS OURSELVES

The Matthew 22:37-39 command to love others as much as we love ourselves uses the familiar Greek verb for love, *agapao*, which we defined in chapter 1 as an action verb. To love someone is to look out for, to take care of, to prefer. We may not feel good about ourselves on any one day of the week, but the vast majority of us will take care of our own needs before those of another.

Listed below are some ways we may love ourselves more than we love our neighbors. *Remember*, to love another means to treat another as well as we treat ourselves.

1. In the seven actions listed below, which one(s) would be the most difficult for you to do?

   Why do you think this is so?

   a. Do you excuse your neighbor's behavior as graciously as you excuse your own? When you arrive late for church, you bless your tardiness with the excuse that the phone rang at the last minute or because you're overworked and needed a few more winks of sleep. If a neighbor shows up late for church, you might label her inconsiderate and disruptive as she climbs over you to get to her seat, never stopping to think her reason for being late may be better than yours. When you say unkind words to your spouse or children, you excuse yourself because of your exhaustion or your difficult day. Your neighbor says unkind words and you may label him judgmental and mean-spirited.

   b. Do you accept your neighbor's emotions as easily as you accept your own? When you're depressed, it's because your family situation is difficult, the dog died or your mother is ill. Your neighbor gets depressed and you accuse the neighbor of self-pity. Your anger is usually justified; your neighbor's anger reveals his or her immaturity.

c. Do you guard your neighbor's good reputation as carefully as you guard your own? You don't gossip about yourself. However, you may not hesitate to tell your friends about the lazy mother who sleeps in and lets her children fix breakfast, a coworker who chats on the phone with friends during work hours, or a friend who often forgets luncheon engagements or your birthday celebration.

d. Do you take actions to insure that your neighbor is as well fed, clothed and housed as your own family? If your neighbors are unemployed and without benefits, do you share your paycheck so the family may pay their bills, buy groceries and clothing with the same ease with which you pay for yours? Would you be willing to cancel your Colorado ski trip in order to bless a missionary friend with desperately needed funds?

e. Do you try to anticipate and meet your neighbor's unspoken needs in the same way you want yours to be anticipated and met? If your neighbor is painting or wallpapering, do you offer to help? If your neighbors are moving, do you offer to help them pack the truck or to serve them breakfast on the day of their move without being asked?

f. Do you give up your planned activity to join in the activity desired by your closest neighbor? Your closest neighbor may be your spouse, your child, a friend or a relative. If you can't possibly think about missing the ball game but your spouse wants you to attend the home and garden show, which activity would you choose?

g. Do you forgive your neighbor as readily as you forgive yourself? If you dent the front fender of your car, you probably won't hold a grudge against yourself. But if your neighbor borrows your car and dents the fender, you might mentally or verbally accuse him or her of driving carelessly or too fast.

2. Name other ways we fail to treat others as graciously, kindly or generously as we treat ourselves.

A Closer Look at God's Truth

Read Matthew 22:37-39.

> Jesus replied, "'Love the Lord your God with all your heart and with all your soul and with all your mind.' This is the first and greatest commandment. And the second is like it: 'Love your neighbor as yourself.'"

According to Jesus, how many commandments are there in this quote? Two, of course. But if you count loving yourself a commandment, you end up with three commandments.

3. Read the following scripture. Does God's Word assume that men love their bodies or need to be trained to love their bodies?

> In this same way [as Christ loved the church], husbands ought to love their wives as their own bodies. He who loves his wife loves himself. After all, no one ever hated his own body, but he feeds and cares for it, just as Christ does the church (Ephesians 5:28,29).

Scripture maintains that Christian love is best demonstrated in our actions, not our words.

4. Read Matthew 25:31-40. The goats seem puzzled by their separation from the sheep. What kind of churchgoers do the goats represent?

5. What does 1 John 3:14,15 say about the seriousness of our relationships with one another? How do you feel as you read this scripture?

6. Read 1 John 3:16-18. What is the one sure way we know that God loves us?

7. Write a definition of love that includes biblical truth on this subject.

Look at *Vine's Complete Expository Dictionary* for a more complete definition of biblical love than we read in chapter 1.

> Love can be known only from the action it prompts. God's love is...an exercise of the Divine will, in deliberate choice, made without assignable cause...Christian love...is not an impulse from the feelings, it does not always run with the natural inclinations, nor does it spend itself only upon those from whom some affinity is discovered...Love seeks opportunity to do good to all men.[1]

A Closer Look at My Own Heart

8. Read Luke 9:23,24. What does it mean to you to take up your cross daily?

Write a definition of self-denial.

9. Circle the letters of each of the following ways you have difficulty in denying yourself:

   a. *Self-importance*—If you walk into a gathering of people wondering who will speak to you, who will notice you, who will remember your birthday or prayer request, you are choosing self-importance. Since Christ calls you to deny self-importance, you need to welcome the lonely, befriend the friendless, listen to the ignored, hug the hurting and pray for the despondent.

   b. *Self-occupation*—If you arrive at a meeting or church gathering with your lists of people to see and things to do, you may be so self-occupied that you ignore the hurting people around you or fail to hear the person telling you she will have surgery the next day.

      To deny self-occupation is to remember to say "Hi, how are you doing?" before you blurt out a question such as "Can you possibly help me with Bible School next week?" Too often we only agree to help people when we are free to choose the time, the place and the way. Unfortunately, people need help when we have made previous plans. Denying self-occupation means letting your wallpapering or yard work wait as you cook a meal for a sick neighbor or mow an elderly person's lawn.

   c. *Self-affection*—If you overtalk about your vacation, achievements or family members at the expense of another's need to talk, you are allowing self-affection to ruin your listening skills. How well do you listen? Do you listen so that you may find a time to turn the conversation back on yourself, or do you listen to understand what the other person is saying?

   d. *Self-protection*—Your ego wants to defend itself against criticism and correction. When you are in the self-protective mode, you will criticize the person who dared to criticize you: "The way she treats her husband, how dare she tell me I've wronged mine." If you don't self-protect, you will often raise yourself above the one criticizing you: "I certainly won't listen to anything spoken that harshly and without love."

e. *Self-inspection*—Often we check our feelings to see if we should attend church, read the Bible or say yes to sex with our spouse. How much wiser it is to check your decisions or commitments. God calls you to live in obedience to His Word and His Spirit; He does not call you to obey your emotions.

f. *Self-sufficiency*—God has decreed an interdependent lifestyle for believers. We are members of one another (see 1 Corinthians 12:27). Is it difficult for you to allow another to change a tire on your car when you have a backache, or to clean your house, rake your lawn or care for your children when you are ill? Do you find it difficult to ask for help or refuse offered help when you need to receive it? To deny self-sufficiency is to admit that you need help and will receive it when offered.

What examples can you add to this self-denial list?

10. Read John 13:34,35 and Romans 13:8-10. List the reasons you find for loving your neighbors as you love yourself.

Action Steps I Can Take Today

11. What one thing can you start to do today to stimulate your growth in self-denial such as accepting offered help when you need it?

To grow in self-denial this week, with God's help I will:

Notes:
1. W. E. Vine, *Vine's Complete Expository Dictionary* (Nashville, Tenn.: Thomas Nelson Inc., 1984), pp. 381-382.

- Three -

HONORING ONE ANOTHER

———◦/◦/◦———

I can still remember the office where the professional counselor and I sat. There was a restrained stillness before she spoke her question. "Bobbie," she asked as she leaned forward to touch my hand, "do you by chance have an exaggerated sense of self-importance?"

Ouch! I knew my counselor would not have asked unless she felt I suffered from a bloated sense of self-importance. I didn't answer. Instead, I took the question home with me. After days of self-pity and denial, I finally accepted the question as legitimate. I decided to spend time in prayer to receive the Holy Spirit's illumination of any truth behind this probing question. In His time, God showed me my incessant need to speak in every committee meeting and every Bible study I attended; how I blocked every driver who dared to try and cut in on me; my impatience in listening to others speak, causing me to interrupt so I could talk; my expecting my opinions to be accepted as "the truth"; my tendency to elevate self by announcing to others my good deeds that God wants me to forget, send on to heaven and wait for His reward.

Acknowledging failures isn't fun, but the first step toward change is realizing where we are failing. When the scales of blindness fall off, we see ourselves as others do. That's exhilarating! This Bible study provides a time to stretch our faith and acknowledge our failures. As you study how to honor one another, remember that the Lord compassionately corrects while the enemy fiercely condemns.

A Closer Look at the Problem

THE JOY OF BEING HONORED
I appreciate some of the strong synonyms Roget lists for the word "honor" in his thesaurus: "acclaim, admire, appreciate, compliment, lionize, look up to," etc. I remember a time when I felt blessed in all these ways by a reception given in my honor by a Bible study group I had taught for thirteen years. The women honored me with a scrapbook of more than a hundred letters of appreciation; The Bible Study Core Group took the time to uncover funny incidents in my life and presented a "This Is Your Life, Bobbie" skit. There was the corsage, the decorations, poems, tears and laughter. But what I appreciated most was each woman who interrupted her busy schedule to attend the reception and write a loving letter in appreciation of me. I truly felt lionized.

1. Think of a special time in your life when you felt honored. What made the event so special to you? Recall all the emotions you felt at this time and why you felt them.

2. Describe a time when you honored a friend or family member.

A Closer Look at God's Truth

THE ATTITUDE OF LOVE
In chapter 2 we looked at the *actions* of love. Today we focus our attention on the *attitude* of love. This lesson will place a magnifying glass over the commandment found in Romans 12:10: "Outdo one another in showing honor" (*RSV*) or "in honor let each set his neighbor above himself" (*The Epistles of Paul*, W. J. Conybeare).

In this chapter we will study the meaning of the original Greek word for honor, search the Scripture for people we are to honor and learn specific scriptures that instruct us how to honor others.

The Godhead is our role model for considering others more important than ourselves.

3. Read John 14:13; 15:26 and 17:24 and record how the members of the Godhead glorify each other.

4. When you are part of a group, what are some things you do to call attention to yourself?

5. What are some specific things you might do to call attention to others, as the members of the Godhead do for one another?

6. Read Romans 12:10. Whom should you honor? The word "honor" in your Bible translation might be value, esteem, respect, etc.

In most translations of the Bible, you will find the noun form of the Greek word for honor translated "price." We know the great value God places on us when we realize the enormity of the price He paid to make us His own:

> For God has bought you with a great price. So use every part of your body to give glory back to God, because he owns it (1 Corinthians 6:20, *TLB*).

In 1 Peter 2:17 we are told to honor everyone, which would include the poor and the rich; the common man and the king; the ignorant and the educated; people without positions and people with positions; dirty, smelly people and clean, neat, perfumed people.

7. In the world's view, what things make a person worthy of honor?

8. Read Genesis 1:26,27 and Psalm 8:3-9 and compare the world's reasons for honoring others with God's reasons for honoring all people.

We honor all women and men because we are original, one-of-a-kind masterpieces, created by the Master Artist of the universe in His image. When we honor others, we are honoring their Creator. When we dishonor others, we dishonor God.

SPECIFIC PEOPLE WE ARE TOLD TO HONOR

9. Read the following scriptures. Beside each listed scripture, identify the persons we are told to honor.

Philippians 2:25,29,30

1 Timothy 5:3

1 Timothy 5:17

1 Timothy 6:1,2

1 Peter 2:17

1 Peter 3:7

10. In what ways was this list of honored men and women unusual for first-century society and even for today?

What a fresh word of hope these scriptures must have brought to first-century wives, widows and common people—the *least* members of society. Today, this would be the same as telling us to honor homeless people. Notice that the passage in 1 Peter lists all people as worthy of honor before it singles out the king. The Christian faith is revolutionary in commanding us to honor the least significant members of society because of their intrinsic worth as people created by God.

WHAT ABOUT OUR SALTINESS?

11. Beside each of the following scriptures, write specific ways we are told to honor others.

Leviticus 19:32

Romans 16:16

1 Corinthians 11:33

1 Peter 4:9

1 Peter 5:5

12. One way we honor one another is by being polite and showing courtesy toward one another. Unfortunately, we can see a noticeable decrease in civility and an increase in rudeness in our society.

    Name some of the manners most parents used to teach their children that few parents teach children today.

Although the following examples may seem trivial or superficial today, the following behaviors are outward signs of a wide-ranging breakdown of respect and increase of selfishness. Men and children no longer stand when a woman enters the room. Doors are no longer held open for women or the elderly. Some women even scorn the common courtesies that men traditionally performed, leaving males bewildered about what today's women want. Recently I sat on the floor of a Sunday School class while none of the men present offered this 67-year-old woman a chair. Children are no longer taught to respect their elders. How many families wait and have blessing before anyone starts to eat? How often is the gift of hospitality exercised in Christian homes today?

POOR LISTENING SKILLS

A teenage girl once confided to me, "Everyone I try to talk to at our church coffee hour keeps looking over my shoulder to see who they can talk to next." This young woman felt deeply rejected by church members and later attempted suicide. Our body language and tone of voice quickly communicates to another our respect or disrespect.

Scripture assumes we like to talk. It never encourages us to talk more, but instead in Proverbs 18:13 we are told it is shameful behavior to speak before listening. James 1:19 commands us to listen before speaking. All too often we listen to speak instead of listening for understanding. We listen with our answers running in our heads, waiting to add our two cents worth to the conversation.

When we listen without interrupting, when we stay focused on the subject the speaker has introduced instead of turning the conversation on ourselves and what we want to talk about, we honor the other person. You may be amazed at how difficult it is to learn to listen to understand, instead of listening for the moment when you can interrupt and speak. If you want to have your heart's number one interest revealed, take the "Three Q Test."

A Closer Look at My Own Heart

THE THREE Q TEST

Our listening, or lack of listening, quickly reveals the focus of our hearts. Are we more self-centered than others-centered? A salesman once shared with me his secret of success, "I always ask three questions of my customers before I speak about myself or one of my products." He finds something in the customer's office that indicates a hobby or interest. He then expresses his interest in the customer by asking at least three questions about the customer's family or interests.

The average person, untrained in listening skills, rarely if ever asks three questions about any subject someone *else* introduces. If it's talk about a bright child or darling grandchild, the average listener will ask one question and then say, "You know my granddaughter called me last night to tell me she loved me." If the topic is surgery, again we are good for one or two questions before we say something like, "My father underwent that same surgery last year!" If the talk centers on favorite vacation spots, one question is normal before the listener says, "I was in Hawaii last year! We loved it!"

It's not that we should never talk about our families and our activities, it's just that one of the best ways to honor someone is to show a genuine interest in what the speaker is saying. Try asking someone at least three questions before you say "I" or "we." Here's an example of a listener who honored the speaker with three questions.

> *Speaker:* "I'm speechless with joy! Our first granddaughter was born last week! And she's such a sweetheart."
> *Question One:* "Wonderful! Tell me all about her. Do you have a picture?"
> *Speaker:* "You know I do! Let me show you Grandma's Brag Book."
> *Question Two:* "Such a beautiful baby (while looking at pictures)! Who does she look like?"
> *Speaker:* "My daughter. We compared baby pictures and she's identical to her mother."
> *Question Three:* "Were you there when she was born? I forget where your daughter lives."
> *Speaker:* "Sue is just 50 miles away. I stayed with her for ten days.

We'll be seeing baby Courtney once a week when possible. I just love her."

The "Three Q Test" is one you learn to pass by intentionally counting the questions before you speak. If you spend a day just listening to others at the fitness club, the office, the beauty parlor, the church, you'll discover how seldom people honor another through listening.

Our responses also reveal disrespect for others. Here are four ways to show disrespect:

A. **We are disrespectful when we reject another's feelings and tell the speaker he or she has no right to feel the way he/she does:**

   The speaker: "I feel like I'm a burden to the world lying in this bed helpless and paralyzed."

   Disrespectful Response: "How can you say such a thing? You know you're a blessing to everyone who visits you."
   Respectful Response: "It must be really tough having to ask everyone to do for you when you'd like to be doing for yourself."

B. **We are disrespectful when we challenge the speaker's perception of a controversial issue:**

   The speaker: "Vitamins are the best cure to date found for cancer."

   Disrespectful Response: "That's hocus-pocus, the most stupid thing I've ever heard."
   Respectful Response: "How interesting! Tell me how you came to place so much trust in vitamins."

C. **We are disrespectful when we give cliché answers to a speaker's problem:**

   The speaker: "I'm so worried my son might experiment with sex now that he's in high school."

Disrespectful Response: "It's obvious you're not trusting God."
Respectful Response: "That must be a big concern for you."

D. We are disrespectful when we fail to use "The Three Q Test":

The speaker: "My son just made starting quarterback on his high school team."

Disrespectful Response: "That's nice. My son just made the honor society."
Respectful Response: "I'm sure you're proud of him. How long has he played football? Is he a junior or senior this year? Does he plan to go on with his football career in college?"

13. Write down the ways you would welcome Jesus if He dropped by during your Bible study.

Can we do less for anyone God places in our lives? Remember, whenever we honor the least of society we honor Jesus Christ our Lord (see Matthew 25:35-40).

Action Steps I Can Take Today

14. Ask yourself: Do I honor people because of their position, wealth and knowledge or because they are divine originals, created by the Lord of the universe?

Do I listen with my answers running in my head or do I listen to understand?

15. Practice respectful answers to the following by writing down how you should respond, using the *A* through *D* examples on pages 34-35:

    A. *Speaker:* "I feel like a real nut forgetting my lines in the church play. I'm so embarrassed."
    Respectful Answer:

    B. *Speaker:* "I believe the Bible is a book of fairy tales."
    Respectful Answer:

    C. *Speaker:* "I know I'm going to get the flu that's going around."
    Respectful Answer:

    D. *Speaker:* "I got an A+ on my math test!"
    Respectful Answer:

To show respect for the speaker, respond to what is true in what he or she says. To see how well you have done, check your answers with the following. You're not expected to write the same answers but to reply in the same spirit.

A.   *Respectful Answer:* "It must have been hard for you to stick in there when you felt like running off the stage and never returning." (Disrespect would challenge the speaker's emotions: "Well, that's the silliest thing I ever heard. It was only a church play.")

B.   *Respectful Answer:* "I'd be interested to know more about your biblical studies that led you to that conclusion. Did you study alone or did you go to Bible school?" (Disrespect would put down the speaker's conclusions: "If you'd really studied the Bible, you wouldn't say such a thing.")

C.   *Respectful Answer:* "This year's flu seems to be of a more serious variety. Have you been exposed to it?" (Disrespect would trivialize the speaker's worry and also give a cliché answer: "Why would you say such a thing like that? What we fear always comes upon us.")

D.   *Respectful Answer:* "That's wonderful. Which math class are you taking? Who is your teacher? How much studying did you have to do? You must feel good doing so well after all your hard work." (Disrespect would turn the conversation back on self: "That's nice. Math was my most difficult subject, but I managed to make straight *A*s.")

16.   To whom do you need to show honor? What one thing could you do this week to show that person honor?

17.   Plan how you will put these new listening skills into practice this week.

Four

ENCOURAGING ONE ANOTHER

The Words Love Speaks

I remember little from my childhood, but one event stands chiseled in my memory. At age eight God miraculously healed me from a kidney disease the doctors said would probably be fatal. After nine months of bed rest I returned to church, stepping out of the car wobbly on my toothpick legs. Many members of our small church rushed up to give me a warm, but general greeting such as, "Oh, it's so good to have you back." But Mrs. Meadows, a missionary friend, took my hand in hers, stooped down to look me directly in my eyes and said, "Bobbie Lee, God saved you for a very special purpose." My life was touched by God through Mrs. Meadows. She encouraged me in the Lord.

We have studied the actions and attitudes of love. In this chapter we examine *the words* love speaks. Psychologists estimate that each day we have about seven hundred opportunities to speak. Talkative people utter about twelve thousand sentences a day which averages out to approximately one hundred thousand words.

A DAILY SPEECH CHECKUP

How many of our words are encouraging? How many are discouraging? The Bible tells us that we will be held responsible for every careless word we speak (see Matthew 12:36,37). God's Word clearly instructs us to encourage one another daily (see Hebrews 3:13) and speak only words that build up others (see Ephesians 4:29).

Are your words mostly positive or negative? We'll discover fresh, new ways to encourage those whose lives touch ours and appreciate together our God, the God of *all* encouragement.

1.   I estimate that _____ percent of my words are negative and discouraging, and _____ percent of my words are encouraging to others.

A Closer Look at the Problem

Before we learn some of the many ways to encourage another, let's look at the enemy of encouragement. The enemy is *criticism*, the discourager. We need to remind ourselves that criticism changes no one and often becomes counterproductive. (If it worked, think how nice we'd all be!) Criticism ranks highest in the arsenal of people weapons.

I believe we must avoid a backward look at poor behavior and instead tell the child or adult what we'd like to see happen. For example:

Poor: "How many times do I have to tell you to wipe your shoes on the mat before coming in the house?"
Good: "Stephen, please go back and wipe your feet on the mat."

Poor: "Why do I have to tell you a hundred times that the washing machine's leaking? Can't you ever put my needs on the top of your 'to do' list?"
Good: "Honey, the washing machine is leaking so much I'm afraid it might ruin our floor. I'd really appreciate your coming to see what you can do as soon as this last load finishes spinning."

Poor: "I'd appreciate one decent dinner a week. Can't you ever come up with something better than TV dinners?"

Good: "Honey, do you think we could have one of your delicious cooked dinners tonight? I'll clean up if you'll cook."

OUR WORDS HAVE POWER

The Bible tells us the power of life and death is in our words (see Proverbs 18:21). When discouraged by criticism, I overeat and hold a pity party to which I invite no one but myself. A dangerous downward spiral of negative thinking begins with my telling myself "I never do anything right. I'm ineffective in the kingdom of God, and no one likes me." Too often I allow one perceived failure or one critical remark to trigger depression.

I used to neglect filing my fingernails until one day a friend noticed that I had filed them. She took my hands in her lovely manicured ones and exclaimed, "Bobbie, you fixed your fingernails! How nice they look!" Ever since (with an occasional slip) I have filed my nails. Our words have power. We can help create change in every life that touches ours by looking for something to praise and then speaking it out daily. *But one word of caution:* Just as we want to criticize actions and not people, we want to praise actions and not people. If you say, "You are the nicest person in the world!" the recipient of the praise may mentally refuse the exaggerated compliment, thinking instead of all the people nicer than he or she. How much better to say, "I appreciate your warm greeting and friendly smile."

Poor: "You are the most faithful Christian I know."

Good: "I appreciate your faithfulness in teaching the Bible all these years."

REASONS FOR CRITICISM

We criticize for many reasons:

a. Our parents may have earned graduate degrees in negativity while raising us.

b. The newspapers, Internet and TV daily drench our minds with global accounts of diabolic events.

c.   We may subconsciously criticize others as a way of building up ourselves. When we say "Thomas never brings his wife flowers," we
imply that we would not dare to be so insensitive to forget to honor
our wives with flowers.

d.   To encourage others costs us something. In order to build them up, we
have to set self aside.

Regardless of how little we know about encouragement and how few role
models we find, we can learn to "encourage one another daily, as long as it is
called Today" (Hebrews 3:13).

A Closer Look at God's Truth

THE WORD "ENCOURAGE"

If you look up the words "encourage," "exhort" and "comfort" in a New Testament concordance or a Greek dictionary of the New Testament, you will
discover that there is only one Greek verb for all three translations. The word
is *parakaleo*, which means "a calling to one's side." The Holy Spirit is called the
parakletos because He is the one who comes beside to help, comfort and encourage us.

2.   Read the following scriptures in as many translations as possible and list
the different verbs used to capture the richness of the verb "to call to one's
side."

John 11:19

1 Thessalonians 5:11

Hebrews 3:13

3. In the following scriptures we find the noun, *paraklesis,* "the one who comes to help." Read the following passages in as many translations as possible to discover the different words used for an encourager.

   John 14:16

   Acts 4:36

   2 Corinthians 1:3

4. Based on these scriptures, write what you think the Bible means when it tells us to encourage one another daily.

Encouragement can be conveyed by our physical presence, practical help or in our spoken and written words. An encourager comforts, consoles, exhorts, takes another's side and helps.

5. We can read the Bible from Genesis to Revelation with joy in our hearts because God is the God of all encouragement. Read Genesis 3:14-16,21 and Revelation 21:1-4. In what ways do these scriptures comfort you?

6. List at least two other scriptures that encourage you:

Examples of scriptures that encourage are Romans 8:31: "If God be for us, who can be against us?" (*KJV*) and Philippians 1:6: "Being confident of this, that he who began a good work in you will carry it on to completion until the day of Christ Jesus." How God views His children excites, exhilarates and encourages. Scriptures reveal that our heavenly Father sees us complete in Christ: holy, blameless and glorified saints. God speaks of us today as we will one day be. He knows the power of words (see Romans 8:30; 2 Corinthians 3:18; Colossians 1:2,22 and 1 Peter 2:9,10).

7. Read Hebrews 3:12,13. Why is it crucial to encourage others daily?

We think we have to point out others' faults to keep them from sinning while Scripture tells us we keep others from sinning by encouragement. It is not clear in this passage who benefits from the encouragement: the speaker or the listener. I believe both do.

A Closer Look at My Own Heart

Matthew 12:34 reminds us that "out of the overflow of the heart the mouth speaks." Our words are a belated announcement to the world of what we have been thinking and feeling.

8. Read Ephesians 4:29. Place the stethoscope of this verse to your heart and ask God to reveal any negative patterns of unwholesome speech you might have such as gossip, anger, put-downs or joking at the expense of others:

    Ask Him to also reveal times when you have failed to encourage others:

Action Steps I Can Take Today

9. Here are some ways to encourage others. Circle the letter of one or two of the following ideas you are challenged to try this week:
    a. Pray for others and let them know that you are remembering them. We all are encouraged when people remember our prayer requests and tell us, "You asked me to pray for your father last week. How is he doing?"

b. Tell your children and grandchildren how special they are to the Lord. I read of one mother who whispered into each child's ear as she tucked them in bed, "I know God has a special plan for your life."

c. Speak your positive thoughts to the person who inspired them. Don't just *think* that the speaker is excellent, the choir inspirational, the ushers warm and friendly, or your granddaughter looks great in red, and you're proud of your son's achievements as a Christian, a student, a professional, a father, etc. To encourage more, become aware of your positive thoughts and *verbalize* them—daily!

d. Recognize others' God-given gifts. We may say, "I appreciate what you said in the meeting. It made sense" or "I appreciate the way you get here early to set up the chairs" or "I appreciate your ministry to my children in Sunday School."

e. Stop criticizing others. Try what the late Catherine Marshall did. One day the Lord brought to her mind Romans 14:13: "So let us stop criticizing one another" (*Moffatt*). Her assignment that day was not to speak one negative word all day long. She found it difficult and so will the majority of Christians.

f. Encourage others with notes or phone calls. When people feel down and discover a note of encouragement in the mail, they are uplifted.

g. Spur others on when they want to quit by offering a helping hand. One night when I returned home from an exhausting speaking schedule to get ready for weekend guests, I discovered piles of neat, clean, laundered linens that I needed to be prepared for my guests—a love gift from my upstairs neighbor. Strengthened, I felt I could make it through the weekend.

h. In a group setting, practice encouraging others on their birthdays, anniversaries or any other special days. Every group member tells the "special day" person one thing they appreciate about him or her. The honored person ends up feeling warm and loved.

i. Institute "Family Night" in your household—a night of encouraging one member. All other family members tell the one person being affirmed one thing they appreciate about him or her. Encourage another family member the next week.

Choose one way you will try to encourage others. Write down specifically how you will encourage others this week.

10. Pray daily, using this prayer or one of your own:

Dear Father,
      You are the God of all encouragement and You live in me. I con-
fess that I am quick to criticize and slow to encourage others. I ask
Your forgiveness. May this be a day of bright beginnings for me as
I decide to be the encourager You have equipped me to be through
Your indwelling Holy Spirit. In Jesus' name, amen.

- *Five* -

HANDLING CONFRONTATION

If you have a problem with another person, how are you most likely to handle it? Do you confront the person, avoid the person, talk about the person to a third party, or do you forgive and work toward forgetting?

In this chapter we will learn when to rebuke and when to remain quiet about another's thoughtlessness, ineffectiveness in a job or sin. We'll also consider how to talk over your problem with the one who hurt you. As we speak about confrontation we need to remember that in Scripture we are called to put away criticism, malice, revenge and hurtful words. We are called to put on compassion, kindness, humility, gentleness, patience and love even when rebuking another.

A True Story of Church Gossip

When we avoid confrontation, our first reaction is usually to gossip. This true story of church gossip illustrates the pain, ineffectiveness and damage caused by gossip. For the purpose of this study we will define gossip as "the passing on of negatives about someone when he or she is not present to defend him- or herself."

Many people in Grace Church disliked the way the choir director led the time of informal, contemporary worship. A trained musician, she waved her arms excessively and chatted away between choruses, distracting some from centering on the Lord. And she treated the congregation as a choir instead of people who had gathered to worship.

No one spoke to Miss Smith, the choir director, about the problem. Members complained among themselves and some spoke with the pastor, letting him know that Miss Smith was not their favorite worship leader. The pastor, a nonconfronter, chose to ignore the congregational rumblings against her.

Problems intensified when a new assistant pastor, an experienced song leader, joined the church staff. The senior pastor asked him to lead the informal service of congregational worship without first speaking to Miss Smith. The assistant pastor excitedly agreed, ignorant of the minefield waiting to explode around him. Minutes before Miss Smith entered the sanctuary with the choir the next Sunday, the senior pastor whispered in her ear that the new assistant pastor would replace her as worship leader, starting that day.

She was bewildered, hurt and angry. After worship, she confronted the assistant pastor and accused him of stealing her job. An angry encounter followed, both spoke harshly and then avoided one another.

Finally, the new assistant pastor asked the senior pastor for a full explanation of Miss Smith's anger. After listening to the story, the assistant explained his awkward position. Shortly afterwards, he invited Miss Smith to share her feelings and perspective with him. In listening to her, the assistant pastor realized that she felt deserted and hurt by her friends' lack of support of her as worship leader. The assistant explained to her that she was a popular choir director, but not as popular as a worship leader.

Miss Smith was understandably hurt and disappointed, wishing she had received constructive criticism and an opportunity to change her style of worship leadership, but she was also relieved. Now she understood why her friends seemed distant and unsupportive. The truth hurt, but it also set her free. Healing and restoration happened between the assistant pastor and Miss Smith and between her and her friends.

1. If you had been a church member who disliked Miss Smith's style of worship leadership, would you have spoken to Miss Smith, gossiped about the problem with other church members or gone to the pastor? If you had been the senior pastor, how would you have handled the problem?

A Closer Look at the Problem

WHY WE GOSSIP

Gather together two or three people in the choir room, home or office and it won't be long before someone disappoints, angers, hurts or frustrates someone else. We talk to others about people who have displeased us. We gossip. Gossip, in turn, sows seeds of distrust and gives us negative attitudes toward those whom Christ has called us to love.

Our overarching problem is an inability to handle confrontation. We avoid talking with the one we have displeased or the one who has displeased us. If we refuse to talk about a problem with the person(s) involved, we most often end up gossiping. Gossip is the number one relationship problem in many churches, offices, factories, neighborhoods, etc.

My family and I lived for 13 years in a neighborhood shared with four to eight Christian families. We soon learned what poor confronters we were. For example, when a dog repeatedly turned over all our trash cans we gossiped to each other about the problem instead of speaking with the dog's owner. And, yes, we threw rocks at the dog. The Holy Spirit convicted us of the sin of gossip, which we later labeled as "giving one person a negative filter through which to view another."

Suppose I tell you that Mary Johnson was assigned to help me with cleanup after a large church social, but all she ever did was stand around and talk while I worked. If Mary Johnson is assigned to help you with cleanup next week, you will most likely see her through the negative filter I gave you. You would expect her to talk and not work. I don't know about you, but I have enough problems handling my own negative filters without handling yours as well.

Why then do we gossip?

- Gossip is less threatening than talking face-to-face with the problem person. We take what seems to be the easiest way out only to discover we've stepped into a hornet's nest of trouble.
- The story we retell is usually slanted to make us look good and the other person flawed. We fail to realize the damage we inflict on another's reputation.
- We may use gossip to manipulate people to join our side.
- We gain sympathy for ourselves by telling the dreadful way we have been treated.
- Gossip makes us feel powerful—we know something someone else does not know.
- We have such poor communication skills and often don't know how to talk about a problem without making it worse.

2. What reasons are behind your own gossiping?

This chapter will help us evaluate our options for solving relationship problems. The principles shared must be applied to your individual situation asking for the Holy Spirit's guidance in prayer.

A Closer Look at God's Truth

WHAT SCRIPTURE SAYS ABOUT GOSSIP

3. Read Proverbs 16:28. What other problems are caused by gossip?

4. Read Proverbs 20:19. How are we to treat a gossip?

5. Read 2 Corinthians 12:20. What cluster of problems does Paul list with gossip?

6.   Read 3 John 9,10. How did John handle gossip?

Scripture teaches us that gossip not only separates good friends, but also brings anger, strife and quarreling. Gossip is the work of Satan and a primary weapon he uses to destroy Christian fellowship.

7.   Read Ephesians 4:15,25,29. If the people involved in the choir director's story had obeyed these verses, what hurts could have been avoided?

8.   Give an example of when you have spoken in love even when it may have hurt the listener. If you cannot think of an example of speaking in love, describe a time when you were afraid to confront someone. What were the results of not confronting that person?

Give an example of when you created a secondary problem by avoiding the first problem, as the pastor did. What happened as a result?

What do you think the pastor should have done when the first person complained to him about Miss Smith?

In one church I've heard about staff members covenanting together to stop all gossip about church members and other staff members. Wow! That's a humbling, yet powerful, decision with the promise of the Holy Spirit revolutionizing and empowering the entire church. If you sometimes or often speak to a third party about a problem person, instead of to the person, pause now for a moment of prayer. Ask the Holy Spirit to reveal the reasons behind your behavior.

WHAT SCRIPTURE SAYS ABOUT REBUKING

9.   Read Psalms 39:11 and 50:16-21. When does God rebuke people?

10. Read Proverbs 15:31,32. In what ways do these scriptures encourage us to rebuke when necessary?

11. According to Matthew 18:15-17, what is the godly way to rebuke a fellow Christian?

12. Read Matthew 23:23-36 and 1 Peter 2:21-23. What caused Jesus to give a sharp rebuke in the first situation while in the second He remained silent?

Jesus sharply rebuked anyone who sinned against God or led others into sin. He never defended Himself against personal attack. This is a powerful position to take against others' rebukes of us.

13. There are times to rebuke and times not to rebuke a fellow Christian. Read Galatians 2:11-16; 1 Timothy 5:1,20; 2 Timothy 3:16; 4:2 and Titus 2:15. Invest time in reflecting on these scriptures and summarize what you have learned about giving a rebuke.

Before rebuking a sinner we need to decide if his or her actions have drawn others into sin. Paul publicly rebuked Peter because others had followed his example by refusing to eat with Gentiles. This legalistic behavior could not be tolerated in the new church community.

In rebuking another it's wise to select the time, place and choice of words prayerfully. With noninflammatory words, free of accusation and judgment, we must speak in a neutral tone of voice.

> *Poor:* "You are a gossip and troublemaker. I am sick and tired of your causing dissension in the church."
> *Better:* "Betty, I have some difficulty with what you just shared with me. I don't like to hear gossip. It gives me a negative view of my fellow Christians whom I'm supposed to love. Why don't you talk with this person and see if you can work things out between the two of you?"

If we compare the number of times in God's Word we are told to love one another with the number of times we are told to admonish or rebuke, we'll see that Scripture emphasizes unconditional love. When we totally accept others in love and with prayers for the thorn in our side, the Holy Spirit is free to correct and convince the other of thoughtless or sinful behavior. Our criticism usually changes no one.

We may challenge these instructions, pointing to the example of Jesus who rebuked sinners harshly. But He was God's Son—without sin! Let's rebuke in a way that gains an audience with the other person and makes it as easy as possible for him or her to repent.

HOW TO ADMONISH

How does an admonishment differ from a rebuke? The emphasis of a rebuke is "You have sinned" while the emphasis of admonishment is "Let me tell you what the Bible says about this problem." Admonishment in the Greek means "a putting in mind." And with the help of the Holy Spirit we are capable admonishers. The Bible says:

> I myself am convinced, my brothers, that you yourselves are full of goodness, complete in knowledge and competent to instruct one another (Romans 15:14).

A Closer Look at My Own Heart

14. Think of a situation where you may need to admonish someone. Ask yourself each of the following questions about this situation. Decide what you should do about admonishing this person. What will you do about this situation this week?

    a. **Do I have the grace to overlook this behavior and not talk to anyone else about it?** If so, I will forgive and forget. Mary Johnson's unhelpful kitchen behavior could have been handled with a kind, upbeat admonishment, spoken directly to Mary: "Mary, I really need to finish with this cleanup and get home. Could you come and help?"

b. **Will this person's behavior hurt only me?** If so, I will not admonish, remembering, "A man's wisdom gives him patience; it is to his glory to overlook an offense" (Proverbs 19:11).

c. **What are my motives?** Do I have the other person's best interest at heart, or do I want to straighten out his or her behavior because I am irritated? If I cannot correct in love, I will not speak.

d. **Is this an opportunity to forgive others as God forgives me?** Is my judging attitude the problem rather than the other person's behavior? If so, I will not speak.

Remember, gossip destroys fellowship; correction gains more favor than a flattering tongue. Let us speak the truth in love, knowing that we cannot protect people from pain. Pain is as much a part of relationships as laughter.

Action Steps I Can Take Today

15. Reread the reasons for gossip given on pages 49-50.

16. Spend time in prayer, asking the Holy Spirit to bring to mind specific times when you have gossiped. As you reflect on these incidents, jot down possible motives.

17. If gossip is a sin in your life, you need to confess and repent. To repent does not mean to feel sorry for what you have done. It's great if you do! However, true repentance is a decision to stop, turn around and start walking in a new direction. It means you realize the seriousness of your sin and through God's empowerment you will turn your back on gossip and stop doing it.

18. If you have a repeated pattern of gossip, such as talking with your sister about your mother or talking with one coworker about another coworker, talk to the person with whom you most often share negatives. Tell him or her about your decision to stop gossiping, and ask this person to forgive you for involving him or her in gossip and to remind you when you slip up.

Six

BEFRIENDING OUR EMOTIONS

As a Christian, have you ever condemned yourself for feeling: angry at a friend, depressed about life, or indifferent toward reading the Bible or worshiping God?

Many Christians are so uncomfortable with their emotions that they feel guilty when feeling anything but good. In this chapter we'll learn the biblical way to handle our negative emotions by studying God's dealings with the emotions of Cain, David, Jonah and Job. Relationships wither and die or take root and grow in the "potting soil" of our emotional life. This lesson challenges us to receive our emotional makeup and those of others as God's good gift.

A Closer Look at the Problem

SOME SCARY THINGS ABOUT EMOTIONS

We can shut off our unwelcome thoughts by singing, praying, reading a good book or talking to a friend. We can decide to speak our thoughts or keep quiet. But try as we may, our feelings resist control. Joyous emotions escape like helium from a balloon, while our negative emotions burrow into the dark corners of our heart and resist all change. Life feels out of control when we can't control our (or others') emotions. Fear adds to our confusion.

We fear what others will think if our emotions are exposed. We don't want to look foolish or be judged childish. At the core of our fears are our basic misunderstandings about the role our emotions play in life. These are my basic discoveries about emotions after decades of study:

- Emotions are our initial, involuntary response to a situation or person.
- Emotions are neutral, neither good nor bad, right nor wrong, silly nor sensible.
- Emotions resist change. When we wish to feel happy, we may feel sad. When everyone wants to celebrate, we might feel like crying. Because of feeling out of control when emotions won't obey our commands, we sometimes build a thick inner wall of protection to keep us from feeling anything, or we bury unpleasant emotions deep in the pit of our stomachs—only to suffer from stomach acid. These are dangerous choices with far-reaching future consequences:
  - If we build up our wall to keep out certain emotions, we risk losing all emotions—pleasant or painful. We risk becoming shut down, unable to experience life to the fullest.
  - Buried emotions refuse to stay buried. As author John Powell writes, "When I repress my emotions, my stomach keeps score."

1. Recall a time when someone else's emotions stimulated your anger or fear. How did you respond?

2. Recall a time when life felt out of control because you couldn't control your emotions. How did you respond?

A Closer Look at God's Truth

If we take an overview of scriptures dealing with emotions, we may be better able to accept our emotions as God's good gift to us.

3.   Read Genesis 4:2-8. Describe God's attitude toward Cain's emotions.

4.   What warnings did God give Cain about his negative feelings?

5.   What does this passage teach us about how to handle emotions?

God did not condemn Cain for being angry and depressed. In questioning Cain about his emotions (see v. 6), God possibly wanted Cain to openly discuss his emotions. But Cain refused God's offer. Only after acknowledging Cain's emotions did God warn him that sin was knocking at his door. Cain's emotions were not his sin, but how he chose to handle his emotions led him to sin. Instead of talking with God about his emotions, Cain chose to focus his anger on his brother and probably accused Abel of causing his anger. When we refuse to own—take responsibility for—our emotions and blame another, resentment intensifies, anger builds and people stop speaking to one another. In extreme cases we might verbally, or even physically, murder the one we blame for making us feel so depressed and angry.

6.   Ask God to search your heart and enable you to acknowledge any one you are resenting at this time. Do you blame this person for your emotions? What has this led to: i.e., separation, accusations, brooding, etc.?

      The healthiest way to handle emotions is to say "I am feeling angry" instead of "You make me angry." Which do you usually say?

7.   Read Jonah 3:10—4:11 and answer the following questions:

      Did God condemn Jonah for being angry? What was God telling Jonah about his anger?

Do you think Jonah would have wanted to die if he had talked to God about his feelings? Explain your answer.

8. Read Ephesians 4:26,27. What does Paul tell us is the greatest danger we face when we have negative feelings toward another?

9. Recall some times in your life when you held onto your anger and resentment and did not forgive the person who hurt you until days, weeks, months or years after the day of the emotional event. In what ways, if any, did the devil gain a foothold over your life during that time?

10. Read Mark 3:5; Luke 19:41 and John 13:21. List the emotions Jesus experienced in these passages.

11. Read Exodus 20:5 and Numbers 11:10. What are the two negative emotions God feels?

12. What conclusions about emotions can you draw from reading these passages?

Here's my list of biblical learning about emotions:
- The fabric of life is woven with the warp and woof of positive and negative emotions. We cannot expect to feel good all the time.
- The Bible does not condemn emotions. The sin is not in the possession of emotions but in the expression and actions we take in response to our feelings.
- God encouraged Cain and Jonah to get their eyes off their problems and focus on Him who is the answer. God wanted them to talk with Him

about their feelings, to express their emotions to the divine Listener. If they had, they would most likely have been freed to live life above their anger and depression.

• We need negative emotions. Fear keeps us from taking foolish risks. Depression may signal a need for withdrawal and rest. Anger is an indicator of possible problems. These emotions are signals, like red lights blinking on the dashboard of a car. They call us to stop and lift "the hoods" of our lives and let God examine us until we find out *why* we are experiencing these emotions. We will then learn about our hidden problems of insecurity, rejection of self, resentment against God, bitterness, unforgiveness, lack of faith, etc.

13. Read Psalm 6. What emotions did David express to the Lord in this psalm?

When he expressed his emotions what changes took place in his outlook?

14. Read Psalm 13. What emotions did David express in this psalm?

These psalms begin with David feeling separated from God and end with his affirmation of knowing God had heard him. He moved from a man of sorrow, feeling forgotten by God, to become a man of celebration, singing to the Lord.

15. Jot down any ideas that you learned from David that might help you handle your negative emotions easier.

In a twinkling of an eye, David's emotions seem to do an about-face. He bemoans one moment and the next he sings to God. If I expect the same instantaneous change in my life, I might open myself to discouragement and depression.

When I'm angry, hurt, disappointed or sad about a relationship failure, I go to the Lord and pour out my negative emotions. Like David, I am blunt and colorful in describing in prayer to my heavenly Father exactly how I feel; I journal my feelings and sometimes write a psalm. Often my emotions dwindle in intensity. I take a deep breath of gratitude, rejoice and shout, "I'm free!" only to discover that the demon of resentment has returned, uninvited. I believe the psalms condense days of anguish into a moment of expression. While on this earth we'll never know for sure how many days of wrestling with God preceded the peace of God settling over David's heart.

Getting free of negative emotions is a process with me. Whenever old, negative emotions toward another resurface, I use them to draw closer to God. Instead of condemning myself for this recurrence—which leads to separation from God—I repeatedly cry out to God, "Be my love for Susie. I'm bankrupt of warm feelings toward her. Please let your love flow through me to her." This simple prayer may be repeated multiple times in the days, weeks and months that follow a negative encounter: "Lord, I choose not to become discouraged by the repetition of this prayer. Be my strength. I choose to rejoice that I'm using my negative emotions as a stepping stone to intimacy with and dependence upon my heavenly Father."

MINISTERING TO HURTING PEOPLE

Do you remember how Job, after losing all his flocks, his children, his money and his health, blurted out his overload of negative feelings to his three friends who had come to console him? He moaned:

> "May the day of my birth perish...may God above not care about it... Why did I not perish at birth, and die as I came from the womb...? Why was I not hidden in the ground like a stillborn child...? Why is light given to those in misery, and life to the bitter of soul...? I have no peace, no quietness; I have no rest, but only turmoil" (Job 3:3,4,11,16,20,26).

Then his three friends chided him:

> Eliphaz: "Your words have supported those who stumbled; you have strengthened faltering knees. But now trouble comes to you, and you are discouraged; it strikes you, and you are dismayed. Consider now: Who being innocent, has ever perished? Where were the upright ever destroyed? As I have observed, those who plow evil and those who sow trouble reap it" (Job 4:4,5,7,8).

Bildad: "How long will you say such things? Your words are a blustering wind...if you will look to God and plead with the Almighty, if you are pure and upright, even now he will rouse himself on your behalf and restore you to your rightful place" (Job 8:2,5,6).

Zophar: "If you devote your heart to him and stretch out your hands to him, if you put away the sin that is in your hand and allow no evil to dwell in your tent, then you will lift up your face without shame; you will stand firm and without fear" (Job 11:13-15).

Job blurted out to his friends, "You, however, smear me with lies; you are worthless physicians, all of you! If only you would be altogether silent! For you, that would be wisdom" (Job 13:4,5).

16. In what ways did Job's friends compound his suffering?

17. Have you ever been treated as Job was by his friends? Why do you think we fall into the trap of acting like Job's friends?

How do you want to be treated when emotionally upset?

God did not judge, criticize or correct Job's honest outpouring of every possible dark emotion a man could feel. However, God did chide Job's three friends for their judging words, saying, "I am angry with you...you have not spoken of me what is right, as my servant Job has....[He] will pray for you, and I will accept his prayer and not deal with you according to your folly" (Job 42:7,8).

God, the divine Listener, is the model of how we are to respond to others' shared emotions. It is important that we allow people the full expression of their emotions without judgmental or defensive replies from us.

A Closer Look at My Own Heart

18. Answer the following to yourself:

    Do you tend to correct, criticize or sermonize others' emotions?

    Are you so uncomfortable in the face of honestly expressed emotions that you try to reason away the other's emotions?

    Or do another's expressed emotions reveal your superior spirit when you sit in judgment of the person experiencing deep emotions?

If you do any of the above, prayerfully read and reread the following summary about emotions:

> Emotions that are fully expressed by a hurting person and understood by the listener lose their power over our lives. Emotions that are judged, criticized or corrected intensify and hang around, robbing us of peace and joy.

As we said in chapter 3, listening for understanding requires death to self. Most of us listen to speak and to solve problems. The following illustration and exercise give you practice in listening for understanding.

> If a child screams to her mother, "I hate my sister!" she needs understanding, not sermonizing. If the mother says, "Nice girls don't hate their sisters" the child has learned that she is not nice. She has to handle guilt as well as anger. She may decide never again to tell her mother what she is feeling.
>
> However, if the mother responds with sympathy, saying something like, "It must be hard to live with a sister you hate," the child may open up and share more information about her real problem. She might say, "I don't really hate Amy, but I'm so sick of her getting all the attention. I try and try and never get a part in the play or a solo at church." After the child has expressed her emotions and received a hug from her mother, she is ready to take on life once again with its emotional hurts. She may even want to pray with her mother and thank God for her sister.

19. Try to answer the following remarks without judging, criticizing or correcting.

    a. Johnny returns from school and says, "Everybody on the bus hates me!"
Your accepting response:

If you correct the child and say, "You know that's not true. Craig is your best buddy, and he rides home on the bus with you," Johnny might surprise you by throwing his books on the floor, rushing to his bedroom and slamming the door.

    b. A depressed widow confides: "I want to die! Life is meaningless for me without Daniel."
Your reply:

If you say "Now, Peggy, you know you have lots of important church work to give your life meaning," your friend may wish she had not shared her emotions with you. You are more sympathetic if you say, "I sense your terrible loneliness. After 20 years of marriage, it must be awful to come home to a dark, empty house each night."

Joe Bayly's poignant quote from his book, *The Last Thing We Talk About* says it best:

> I was sitting, torn by grief. Someone came and talked to me of God's dealings, of why it happened, of hope beyond the grave. He talked constantly, he said things I knew were true. I was unmoved, except to wish he'd go away. He finally did. Another came and sat beside me for an hour or more, listened when I said something, answered briefly, prayed simply and left. I was moved. I was comforted. I hated to see him go.[1]

In summary, our emotions in themselves are neither right nor wrong, good nor bad. Sin lies in the way of expression, not in the possession of emotions. When emotionally upset, we can avoid sinning by fully expressing our emotions to

God in prayer or by writing psalms. We can also join God as one who listens to others' emotions without judging, correcting or criticizing. We can help our friends by accepting them with their negative emotions and empathize with them as Paul instructs us to do in Romans 12:15: "Rejoice with those who rejoice; mourn with those who mourn."

Action Steps I Can Take Today

20. In the light of this lesson ask yourself the following:

    a. Do I ever judge myself as less of a Christian because of what I feel? If so, what has this lesson taught me that I need to apply today?

    b. What difficulties do I have in accepting my emotional makeup as God's good gift to me? Review God's attitude toward Cain, Jonah, David and Job from A CLOSER LOOK AT GOD'S TRUTH.

    c. Which one of these reactions—criticism, correction or judgment—is my usual response to the emotions of others? What can I do to improve in listening to others' emotions without criticism, correction or judgment?

    d. Describe what kind of a listener you would like to be. Write out a prayer to God to work through you to make you a divine listener.

Note:
1. Joseph Bayly, *The Last Thing We Talk About* (Elgin, Ill.: Chariot Family Publishing, 1992), p. 29.

- *Seven* -

LEARNING TO LISTEN

St. Francis of Assisi prayed, "Grant that I may not so much seek to be understood as to understand." Unfortunately we often seek the opposite. We prefer to speak, to tell our side of the story, to straighten out every detail of someone else's version of a story that differs ever so slightly from ours.

1. How do you receive criticism from your parents, your siblings, your spouse, your boss or your best friend? Our defensiveness varies, depending on the person correcting or criticizing us and our relationship with that person.

    On a scale of 1 to 10, how would you rate yourself as a nondefensive person, with 10 being extremely self-defensive? _____

I invite you to join me in praying:

> Dear Lord Jesus,
> I am often defensive when accused of wrongdoing. I know and use
> the weapons of denial and counterattack. I speak before listening

fully to another's accusations. At times I let pride keep me separated from a friend. I delay humbling myself, admitting my wrong and asking to be forgiven. Lord Jesus, You humbled Yourself in leaving Your throne in heaven to become a man. Be my humility so I will freely acknowledge where I have been wrong and ask to be forgiven. Amen.

A Closer Look at the Problem

WIN BY LOSING

It doesn't matter if the "something" between two people is large or small, rational or irrational, important or unimportant. If a coolness exists between two members of the Body of Christ, their talking together is essential. And nondefensive listening is the skill most needed at a time like this.

I had to do this one night with a friend. We had both attended a neighborhood worship service held upstairs in our two-family home. When my neighbor's baby cried during those quiet moments of worship and reflection, I remembered that my twenty-one-year-old son was downstairs watching television. I decided to take the baby to him. I walked across the room to where my neighbor stood worshiping and whispered, "I'll take Katy to Craig." I didn't ask her permission and she said nothing. When I returned from delivering the baby to my son's care, I knew I was in trouble. My bubbly, joyful neighbor was scowling, inspecting the floor. I knew she had something against me. I rushed over to speak with her at the close of the meeting, but she rushed out the back door with Katy clutched in her arms.

I was tired and wanted to go to bed. But I knew the message of Matthew 5:23,24:

> Therefore, if you are offering your gift at the altar and there remember that your brother has something against you, leave your gift there in front of the altar. First go and be reconciled to your brother; then come and offer your gift.

My neighbor was one of those beautifully transparent people who shared her emotions openly. If I asked her to tell me how she was feeling, I knew she would. That's why I was going to help set her free of negative emotions by listening nondefensively. I had caused her pain and I was sorry. As I walked to her house, I rehearsed what I would say to my neighbor.

When we sat down to talk, a definite coolness filled the room. Nervously I opened the conversation by saying, "I know I have upset you. I've come to listen to you and try to understand how you felt when I snatched Katy from your arms." After my rehearsed introduction my neighbor boiled over with her version of our encounter.

"You were thoughtless, Bobbie. You didn't stop to think about my feelings or ask me what I wanted done with my baby. You put me in an awkward position."

I felt a knot forming in my stomach, and I longed to shout, "That's not true! I was only trying to help." Instead, I managed to look calmly at my neighbor, swallow and say, "It must have been hard for you. I guess I did appear thoughtless." Notice that I agreed only with the part of my neighbor's speech that was true for me, instead of trying to correct her or defend myself.

"I was ready to take Katy home tonight when you snatched her from my arms. She was tired and needed to go to bed. She didn't need to be taken downstairs to Craig. You know she's afraid of men with beards."

I didn't know men's beards frightened her baby. Again I wanted to defend myself, explain my innocence. I resisted with increased determination.

"I feel you were punishing your son, not helping me," my neighbor accused.

I thought, *My friend, that's enough. You've gone too far.* Instead I miraculously managed to respond to my neighbor's accusation, again accepting the part that was true for me. "I never thought of it that way. You may be right. I was mad at my son," I agreed. "Will you forgive me for my insensitivity and thoughtlessness?" I asked.

With a twinkle in her eyes, my neighbor reached out, hugged me and offered me a cup of coffee. I stayed and talked and went home delightfully free, knowing that for once in my life I had obeyed Jesus' command in Luke 9:23,24, "If anyone would come after me, he must deny himself and take up his cross daily and follow me. For whoever wants to save his life will lose it, but whoever loses his life for me will save it."

If you had kept a tally of points scored, I would have lost. But in losing I won back a friend, practiced humility, learned to listen nondefensively and felt so happy I skipped home at 11:00 P.M.

The pain of the listening process had required that I...

- **Put down pride.** We humble ourselves, admit our wrongs without excusing them and ask to be forgiven. The Bible commands us to: "Be completely humble and gentle; be patient, bearing with one another in love" (Ephesians 4:2). Someone has said, "To be right satisfies my ego; to be humble satisfies God." In giving my friend the gift of nondefensive listening I felt as if I had satisfied God.

- **Refuse to correct.** The object of listening is to be able to say, "I understand why you feel that way," not "You're wrong. It never happened that way." We are able to receive the other person's version of what happened when we realize that feelings are neither right nor wrong. The shared feelings are true only to the sharer. My neighbor later confided to me that it was the first time in her life that anyone had fully listened to her outpouring of negative emotions. She said she was uptight and angry when I walked in, but totally free of all negative emotions when I walked out. Think of the lovely gift we can give by nondefensive listening to a family member or friend when we release self-defense and embrace humility.

- **Cancel all counterattacks.** When we are criticized or corrected, our natural response is to counterattack. We say such things as "Who do you think you are criticizing my tone of voice when you sound like an angry bulldog most of the time." This does not conform to the Bible's teachings, especially the Sermon on the Mount. "But love your enemies, do good to them, and lend to them without expecting to get anything back. Then your reward will be great, and you will be sons of the Most High, because he is kind to the ungrateful and wicked. Be merciful, just as your Father is merciful" (Luke 6:35,36).

A Closer Look at God's Truth

Five more scriptures inspired me to invest the time and practice necessary to become a nondefensive listener.

2. Read Luke 15:18-20. The parable of the prodigal son recounts how a young man returned home to be forgiven after squandering all his inheritance. Before reaching his father's home, he had carefully planned and practiced what he would say to his father. He wanted to get it right!

Contemplate how this young man approached his need for forgiveness. How does he inspire you to make changes in how you handle forgiveness?

The prodigal son's concern centered not on himself but on his father and the pain he had caused him. When we have wronged others, we need to go quickly to them to seek restoration, not exoneration. If we want them to tell us we are still okay, we are excused. But, if we want them to tell us that it wasn't that important, then we are seeking exoneration. In such cases, we want to make up, bypass the problem, skip talking about it. Exoneration, like making up, is external. Restoration, on the other hand, is internal and brings healing. It centers on the relationship between two people and the harm done to it by one's thoughtlessness or sin. The offender comes in humility to say, "I was wrong. I've hurt you and our relationship, and I need you to forgive me." When forgiven by the one you offended, you know you are accepted in your sin, and restoration happens.

3.   Read Matthew 5:23,24. God places a premium on reconciliation and perhaps sees it as more important than worship.

If you procrastinate in asking for forgiveness, what additional problems might you create for yourself?

4.   Read Proverbs 18:13 and James 1:19. Both verses reinforce the need to master listening skills.

What character weaknesses might our tongue reveal about ourselves?

A Closer Look at My Own Heart

5. Describe a time when you put self-protection first and the pain you caused another second.

6. When was the last time you said to someone, "I was wrong. I need you to forgive me"? How difficult was it to say? What was the outcome?

What prevents you from saying, "Forgive me" more often?

Action Steps I Can Take Today

7. Write a defensive and then a nondefensive reply to each of the following accusations. Remember to respond to the part of the accusation that is true for you.
   a. A coworker says: "You were thoughtless yesterday. You embarrassed me when you corrected my spelling in front of the boss."

   Defensive:

   Nondefensive:

   b. A daughter says, "You don't care about me. I don't matter. Tommy gets to do anything he wants and I never get to do anything!"

   Defensive:

Nondefensive:

c. A friend says: "I guess I don't matter to you anymore. You haven't asked me to be your golf partner for months. Yet you've played with Jeff several times in the last few months."

Defensive:

Nondefensive:

Become aware this week of the way you reply to criticism or correction. Examine yourself daily. If you have given a defensive reply, reflect on the encounter and write a nondefensive reply.

Include the prayer on the first page of this chapter in your daily prayers as you ask God to make you one who listens without counterattack.

GROWING IN GRACE

If we would be persons of grace, we must follow the instructions Jesus gave us in the Sermon on the Mount:

> "You have heard that it was said, 'Eye for eye, and tooth for tooth.' But I tell you, Do not resist an evil person. If someone strikes you on the right cheek, turn to him the other also. And if someone wants to sue you and take your tunic, let him have your cloak as well. If someone forces you to go one mile, go with him two miles. Give to the one who asks you, and do not turn away from the one who wants to borrow from you.
>
> You have heard that it was said, 'Love your neighbor and hate your enemy.' But I tell you: Love your enemies and pray for those who persecute you (Matthew 5:38-44)".

We cannot begin to obey these commandments without a big attitude adjustment, which is called "renewing of the mind" in the Bible.

Do not conform any longer to the pattern of this world, but be transformed by the renewing of your mind. Then you will be able to test and approve what God's will is—his good, pleasing and perfect will (Romans 12:2).

In the lesson on emotions in chapter 6, we said that the way we deal with our emotions is a frequent source of people problems. This is true. However, it is not the place to begin when we want to grow in grace and in our ability to respond lovingly to unlovely people. The place to begin is with our thought life. Today, most psychologists agree that emotions flow from our cognitions. We do not feel first and then think; we think first and then emote.

1. If you saw a snake in the road in front of you, coiled and ready to strike, what would you feel? Why would you feel that way?

Your response to the snake would be determined by your self-talk, the things you say to yourself, and the things you have learned over the years. If you thought: *Snakes are dangerous; this snake might kill me*, you would experience the emotion of fear and run for your life. If you were a scientist, however, and thought: *I want to check this snake out; I must get closer and examine its markings and head shape*, you would experience the emotions of excitement and anticipation of learning more about snakes.

This final chapter will stress scriptural thinking as a necessity for right relationships. If we have problem people in our lives, the good news is that we can change the way we *feel* about them by changing the way we *think* about them. In changing the way we think, we adjust our attitude, words and actions and grow as people of grace, capable of returning good for evil.

If we believe that we feel first and then think, we are helpless to change our resentments toward our parents, our anger toward our employers, our disapproval of our pastor, our fear of heights, our jealousy of others' successes or our depression because we haven't fulfilled our lives' dreams. But since life is determined by what we think, we can always change our emotions. We have ready access to our thought life.

A Closer Look at the Problem

2. How would you define the New Testament word "grace"?

There is a richness and depth in this word that we may never fully comprehend. *Vine's Expository Dictionary of New Testament Words* says:

> Grace...[is] the friendly disposition from which the kindly act proceeds, graciousness, loving-kindness, goodwill generally,...especially with reference to the Divine favor of "grace"...: there is stress on its freeness and universality, its spontaneous character, as in the case of God's redemptive mercy, and the pleasure of joy He designs for the recipient.[1]

To me, grace is giving love to the unlovely, forgiveness to the unforgivable, mercy to the unmerciful. In other words, grace is giving a person what he or she does not deserve, which, of course, is how God treats us. God's treatment of Manasseh, king of Judah, is a prime example of divine mercy.

3. Read 2 Chronicles 33:1-6,10-13. What did Manasseh do to deserve God's judgment?

4. In spite of Manasseh's rejection of God, what did God do for him?

5. Describe how you treat people who have ignored, hurt or misused you.

When it comes to people problems, we usually respond in one of three ways:
   a. Like Paul we ask God to remove the problem (see 2 Corinthians 12:7-10).
   b. Like Adam and Eve we blame others for our troubles (see Genesis 3:11-13).

c.   Like Jonah we try to run away from God. We may also try to escape from the people and the problems created by their presence (see Jonah 1:1-3).

How quickly we want to escape our people problems. We want the people removed from our lives or to blame them for our discomfort. God wants us to look to Him and ask, "Father, what am I to learn from this situation? How can I grow in grace toward those who have hurt me?"

Another common way to respond to relationship rifts is to avoid the person giving us trouble. If people have mistreated us, we want to hurt them back and often do so by avoiding them. Ever so subtly (we think), we sit on the opposite side of the church, walk down another aisle in the supermarket or turn our back and talk to others at a gathering. This kind of behavior helps us grow in *disgrace*. Remember, grace is giving others the kindness they do not deserve.

Peter wrote in 2 Peter about the total destruction of the earth and the believer's anticipation of a new heaven and a new earth. Since this is our hope, he challenges us to "grow in the grace and knowledge of our Lord and Savior Jesus Christ" (2 Peter 3:18).

A Closer Look at God's Truth

We have said in previous lessons that God's main concern is not that we have emotions, but that we learn to react to our emotions in a godly way. That's why the first step toward becoming a person of grace is taking charge of our thought life, which leads to a change in our attitude.

6.   Read Philippians 4:8. List the things Christians are called to think about.

When we place our thoughts through the grid of this verse, most of us will agree that we need a mental overhaul. The Bible uses strong action words to let us know how much hard work and discipline are involved in changing our thought patterns.

7.   List some of the biblical commandments about our minds found in the following passages:

Romans 12:2

Ephesians 4:23

Colossians 3:2

1 Peter 1:13

After reading these commands, we see that the Bible insists we can change our thinking. A large percentage of what we think flies in the face of biblical truth; it is sinful and unacceptable to God. We often let Satan's lies replace God's truths.

THE LIES

8. **The Lie:** When people act unfairly, unkindly, thoughtlessly or obnoxiously, I should blame them and dwell on the wrong done to me or to others.

    Use Romans 12:14,17,18 and Ephesians 4:31,32 to rewrite this lie into scriptural truth.

    The Truth:

9. **The Lie:** When I am rejected, hurt or unfairly treated, I have a right to be in a bad mood and harbor negative thoughts.

    Use Matthew 5:11,12 to rewrite this lie into scriptural truth.

    The Truth:

10. **The Lie:** I have a right to criticize and judge other Christians when they fail to obey God's laws. When they don't, I should be depressed.

    Use Matthew 7:1-5 and Galatians 6:1,2 to rewrite this lie into scriptural truth.

    The Truth:

11. **The Lie:** I have a right to expect people to remember me, give me gifts and do special things for me. When they don't, I should be depressed.

    Use Philippians 2:3 to rewrite this lie into scriptural truth.

    The Truth:

12. **The Lie:** I expect people to listen to what's on my mind.

    Use James 1:19,23 to rewrite this lie into scriptural truth.

    The Truth:

If we want healthy relationships, we must discipline our thoughts according to scriptural truth. But all too often when we have been hurt, snubbed, criticized or overlooked, our old natures scream for revenge. We create dramas in our minds based on past painful events. We are the stars of our dramas and have the best lines. We *mentally* "tell off" people who hurt us and "punish" those who cause us pain. The problem intensifies when our mental movies become reruns and then the late, late night shows. Consequently, our emotions match our thoughts; we are plagued with negative, hostile feelings.

13. If you produce emotional home movies in your mind or lose sleep over your late night shows, what can you do to stop the negative, get-even thinking?

When we find ourselves constantly rehashing the same painful memories, it is not helpful to tell ourselves, "I won't think that again." In fact, when we tell ourselves we won't think certain things, we have just thought them a second time. But since our emotions and actions flow from our thoughts, we must be "made new in the attitude of [our] minds" (Ephesians 4:23).

The life of King David illustrates important principles for a healthy thought life with positive emotions and good relationships.

14. Read Psalm 42:1-3 and list the emotions David was feeling.

15. Read Psalm 42:9,10 and describe David's attitude toward God.

16. Read Psalm 42:4-6 and list what David chose to think about, even in his depressed emotional state.

Notice three things about David's thoughts and words:
*   He unabashedly poured out his emotions to God. In telling God exactly how he felt, he seemed to know God as the divine listener of the universe who accepted him with his raw emotions without judging him as flawed.
*   He carefully edited his thought life, choosing to use *replacement thinking*. When he wanted to dwell on his plight in life at the hands of his enemies, he chose instead to remember happy, joyful times of celebrating God.
*   While David seemed to talk freely with God and say exactly how he felt, his self-talk was disciplined and carefully worded. He spoke sharply to his soul, demanding a walk of faith.

We see that when David chose to think of pure, good and true things, his emotions changed. He became a man of hope, knowing he would praise God again as he did in leading the festive procession.

Replacement Thinking

We cannot think about two things simultaneously. This is why replacement thinking proves effective. Instead of saying, "I won't think that again," we need to lift our negative thoughts to God and pray something like:

> Father, I am thinking fearful, negative thoughts again. I give these thoughts to You and ask Your forgiveness for my lack of faith. I repent and choose to think on _____.

It is helpful to decide in advance what you will do when negative thoughts become repetitive. You might choose to pray about your church, every member of your family, your office staff, etc. You can decide to praise God for all His spiritual and temporal blessings. You might quote Psalm 23 or other memorized verses. Notice that I am not saying you will never again have negative thoughts, but when negative thoughts come, we can replace them with positive, scriptural truth. We can use replacement thinking.

Another way to destroy our home movie scripts is to challenge each thought according to Philippians 4:8. It is recommended that we ask ourselves:

> Is this thought noble, right, pure or lovely? Is this thought admirable, excellent or praiseworthy? If not, I will choose to think on _____.

THE UPWARD AND DOWNWARD SPIRALS OF LIFE

Study the following upward and downward spirals. What are their similarities? What are their differences?

6　RELATIONSHIP IS RESTORED, becoming healthy again.

5　MOVEMENT IS TOWARD the person with kindness, conversation, love and a request to be forgiven.

4　FORGIVENESS FLOWS and healing occurs.

3　POSITIVE MIND-SET develops with a rehearsal of Scripture, prayer and praise. The results are the positive emotions of peace, faith and joy.

2　TRUST GOD to be at work in the situation.

1　CHOOSE to see the person/problem as God-sent.

PROBLEM

1　CHOOSE to see/think of a person or problem as an unfair, unwelcome intrusion.

2　MISTRUST GOD and His love and care.

3　NEGATIVE MIND-SET develops with a rehearsal of details, role plays and painful movie scripts. The results are the negative emotions of bitterness, anger, depression, resentment and self-pity.

4　FORGIVENESS is withheld and wounds fester.

5　MOVEMENT IS AWAY from person with gossip, waiting for person to ask forgiveness and blindness to our own wrongs.

6　RELATIONSHIP BREAKS causing emotional and mental pain, sometimes accompanied by physical sickness.

If we do not challenge our thoughts and use replacement thinking when we've been hurt or mistreated, we can get into a downward spiral. If we choose to see the person or problem as God-sent and reaffirm our faith in God, we will experience an upward spiral.

These upward and downward spirals remind us that no matter what happens to us, we can choose how we will respond and think. Time is involved in both spirals; attitudes develop, feelings are affected and relationships are decided.

A Closer Look at My Own Heart

17. Study the upward and downward spirals. Where do you see victory in your life?

Where do you see defeat?

Pinpoint the step that causes you to stumble into a downward spiral.

To be people of grace, we must reach out to others even as they reject us; do deeds of kindness to the ones who hurt us; and refuse to be separated.

Separation of friends is the work of Satan. He knows that if he can keep friends apart long enough, healing will not happen. The longer the separation, the more emotional home movies we produce. Distorted thinking develops. The problem people become monsters in our minds. We come to believe that these people not only hurt us once, but we begin to believe that they are out to destroy us.

Replacement thinking is one solution to distorted thinking. Another solution is to reach out to the ones we most want to avoid. You can call them on the phone, stop by to talk, share a meal or take them a small memento of one of the good times you've spent together. It's vital that we do whatever it takes to bring us face-to-face with the one against whom we hold a grudge. Amazingly, the longer we spend time together the quicker negative feelings dissolve.

18. Have you let a relationship grow cool because you were hurt? Based on this lesson, what steps might you take to try and restore the relationship with the one who hurt you?

19. List any problem people in your life that you need to accept as God's good gift to you.

Action Steps I Can Take Today

20. Use the following worksheet to determine what actions you need to take to restore a broken relationship.

Note:

1. W. E. Vine, *Vine's Expository Dictionary of New Testament Words* (Uhrichsville, Oh.: Barbour & Co., Inc., 1985).

RELATIONSHIP WORKSHEET

a. Stop and pray: "Lord, show me anyone in my family, my church, my neighborhood, my office or factory that I am avoiding. Am I cool toward anyone in my life?" Wait upon the Holy Spirit and listen expectantly. Write down the name of the person who comes to mind.

b. Stop and check yourself: *Have I forgiven this person for his or her thoughtlessness or insensitivity to me? Have I prayed a specific prayer of forgiveness naming the person by name and specifying the hurt to be forgiven?*
   ❏ Yes   ❏ No

> **Note:** Do not move on to step *c* until you can answer yes to question *b*.

c. Ask the Lord to show you one act of kindness you can do for this person you feel like avoiding. It may be anything from baking a cake to sitting by the person at the next choir rehearsal. Pray this prayer:

   Lord Jesus, I ask You to show me one loving act to do for
   _____ (name of person).

   Wait upon the Lord until you decide on one definite act of kindness to help you actively express your new feelings.

d. Make a decision to do this action as soon as possible, trusting in the power of the Holy Spirit to show love through you.

I will _____
                                    (name of action)

for _____
                                    (name of person)

   _____
                      (date)

e. Decide today to ask forgiveness for allowing a rift to develop between you and the person who has wronged you. Go as a humbled person to be forgiven, not as a wronged person to be heard. Like the prodigal son, think about what you are going to say. Write out your request for forgiveness and practice saying it so you can go in humility.

   Here's what I'll say when I go:

What Is Aglow International?

———⦿———

From one nation to 135 worldwide...
From one fellowship to over 3,300...
From 100 women to more than 2 million...

Aglow International has experienced phenomenal growth since its inception 30 years ago. In 1967, four women from the state of Washington prayed for a way to reach out to other Christian women in simple fellowship, free from denominational boundaries.

———⦿———

The first meeting held in Seattle, Washington, USA, drew more than 100 women to a local hotel. From that modest beginning, Aglow International has become one of the largest intercultural, interdenominational women's organizations in the world.

———⦿———

Each month, Aglow touches the lives of an estimated two million women on six continents through local fellowship meetings, Bible studies, support groups, retreats, conferences and various outreaches. From the inner city to the upper echelons, from the woman next door to the corporate executive, Aglow seeks to minister to the felt needs of women around the world.

———⦿———

Christian women find Aglow a "safe place" to grow spiritually and begin to discover and use the gifts, talents and abilities God has given them. Aglow offers excellent leadership training and varied opportunities to develop those leadership skills.

———⦿———

Undergirding the evangelistic thrust of the ministry is an emphasis on prayer, which has led to an active prayer network linking six continents. The vast prayer power available through Aglow women around the world is being used by God to influence countless lives in families, communities, cities and nations.

Aglow's Mission Statement

Our mission is to lead women to Jesus Christ and provide opportunity for Christian women to grow in their faith and minister to others.

———◦◦◦◦———

Aglow's Continuing Focus...

- To reconcile woman to her womanhood as God designed. To strengthen and empower her to fulfill the unfolding plan of God as He brings restoration to the male/female relationship, which is the foundation of the home, the church and the community.
- To love women of all cultures with a special focus on Muslim women.
- To reach out to every strata of society, from inner cities to isolated outposts to our own neighborhoods, with very practical and tangible expressions of the love of Jesus.

———◦◦◦◦———

Gospel Light and Aglow International present an important new series of Bible studies for use in small groups. The first two studies in the Aglow Bible Study Series, **Shame: Thief of Intimacy** *and* **Keys to Contentment***, are available through Gospel Light. Look for these and others in the Aglow Bible Study Series including* **Fashioned for Intimacy Study Guide** *(companion to the book* **Fashioned for Intimacy***)* **Choosing to Change** *and* **God's Character***. For information about these and other outstanding Bible study resources from Aglow, call us at 1-800-793-8126.*

Aglow Ministers In...

Albania, Angola, Anguilla, Antigua, Argentina, Aruba, Australia, Austria, Bahamas, Barbados, Belgium, Belize, Benin, Bermuda, Bolivia, Botswana, Brazil, British Virgin Islands, Bulgaria, Burkina Faso, Cameroon, Canada, Cayman Islands, Chile, China, Colombia, Congo (Rep. of), Congo (Dem. Rep. of), Costa Rica, Côte d'Ivoire, Cuba, Curaçao, Czech Republic, Denmark, Djibouti, Dominica, Dominican Republic, Ecuador, Egypt, El Salvador, England, Equatorial Guinea, Estonia, Ethiopia, Faroe Islands, Fiji, Finland, France, Gabon, the Gambia, Germany, Ghana, Greece, Grenada, Guam, Guatemala, Guinea, Guyana, Haiti, Honduras, Hungary, Iceland, India, Indonesia, Ireland, Israel, Jamaica, Japan, Kazakstan, Kenya, Korea, Kyrgyzstan, Latvia, Malawi, Malaysia, Mali, Mauritius, Mexico, Fed. States of Micronesia, Mongolia, Mozambique, Myanmar, Nepal, Netherlands, Papua New Guinea, New Zealand, Nicaragua, Niger, Nigeria, Norway, Oman, Pakistan, Panama, Peru, Philippines, Portugal, Puerto Rico, Romania, Russia, Rwanda, Samoa (American), Samoa (Western), Scotland, Senegal, Sierra Leone, Singapore, South Africa, Spain, Sri Lanka, St. Kitts, St. Lucia, St. Maartan, St. Vincent, Sudan, Suriname, Sweden, Switzerland, Tajikistan, Tanzania, Thailand, Togo, Tonga, Trinidad/ Tobago, Turks & Caicos Islands, Uganda, Ukraine, United States, U.S. Virgin Islands, Uruguay, Uzbekistan, Venezuela, Vietnam, Wales, Yugoslavia, Zambia, Zimbabwe, plus one extremely restricted 10/40 Window nation.

How do I find my nearest Aglow Fellowship? Call or write us at:

AGLOW
INTERNATIONAL

P.O. Box 1749, Edmonds, WA 98020-1749
Phone: (425) 775-7282 or 1-800-755-2456
Fax: (425) 778-9615   E-mail: aglow@aglow.org
Web site: http://www.aglow.org/

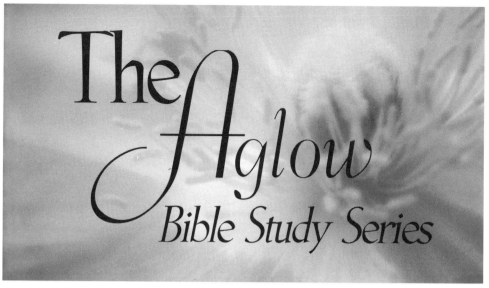

The Aglow Bible Study Series

Shame: Thief of Intimacy
Marie Powers

Powers exposes the characteristics, contributors, and the cure for this emotion that affects women, knowingly or unknowingly, throughout the world.

Paperback • $6.99
ISBN 08307.21290
Available April 1998

Keys to Contentment
Sharon A. Steele

Journey through this study of Paul's life and teachings in his letter to the Philippians and learn how to find the contentment and abundant, joyous life that Jesus promised.

Paperback • $6.99
ISBN 08307.21304
Available April 1998

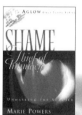

Building Better Relationships
Bobbie Yagel

Use the Scriptures to build successful relationships with your loved ones, friends and neighbors, and learn how to handle confrontations and know when and how to seek forgiveness.

Paperback • $6.99
ISBN 08307.21320
Available July 1998

Choosing to Change
Sharon A. Steele

Overcome rejection, guilt, fear, worry, discouragement and disobedience with the help of four essential steps to renew your mind and transform your life according to Christ.

Paperback • $6.99
ISBN 08307.21312
Available July 1998

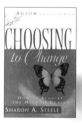

Fashioned for Intimacy
Jane Hansen
with Marie Powers

Jane Hansen, international president of Aglow International, describes God's original design for men and women.

Hardcover • $17.99
ISBN 08307.20669
Available now

More titles in the *Aglow Bible Study Series* are coming soon: two in October 1998 and two in January 1999.

AGLOW
INTERNATIONAL

Gospel Light

Ask for these resources at your local Christian Bookstore.

Let Jane Hansen Lead Your Next Study

Jane Hansen describes the true biblical relationship God yearns to have with each of us. Discover God's original plan for intimacy, and how men and women can be reconciled to Him and each other.

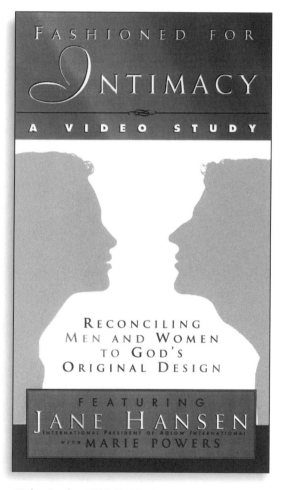

FASHIONED FOR

NTIMACY

A VIDEO STUDY

RECONCILING MEN AND WOMEN TO GOD'S ORIGINAL DESIGN

FEATURING

JANE HANSEN

INTERNATIONAL PRESIDENT OF AGLOW INTERNATIONAL

WITH MARIE POWERS

Video Study • UPC 607135.003649

"*Fashioned for Intimacy* will radically impact the Body of Christ! I highly recommend it to both men and women."

—*Dutch Sheets*
Pastor of Springs Harvest Fellowship
Colorado Springs, CO

"In a time when there is a massive assault coming against the family, resources like this one by Jane Hansen will help to turn the tide of the battle. This is must reading for men and women alike."

—*Rick Joyner*
Morningstar Publications and Ministries

Available at your local Christian bookstore.

Gospel Light